THE OFFICIAL

BALDKNOBBERS

JOKE BOOK

Everybody Loves A Joke!

Printed in the U.S.A. by
Dogwood Printing
P O Box 716 ● Ozark Mo 65721
417-581-8585

Introduction

Everybody loves a joke, and everybody loves to laugh.

When the Mabe Brothers started the **Baldknobbers Show** in 1959, it featured mostly country music, gospel singing and comedy——lots of comedy. Down through the years, hundreds of jokes have been told on the **Baldknobbers** stage. Most of the jokes in this book have been used by the **Baldknobbers** comedians at one time or another.

In this book, you will find the best of the best. If you need a joke for a speech, gathering, business meeting, sermon, or just want a good laugh, you will be able to find it here——Because everybody loves a joke.

A lady was in an accident that required some skin grafting on her face. A skin donor was needed, so her husband volunteered. He couldn't tell her......or show her where they got the skin.........but he couldn't sit down for about two weeks!

The doctor sat her down in front of the mirror and took the bandages off her face. She said to her husband, "Oh honey, I'm pretty again. How can I ever thank you enough?"

He said, "When your mother comes to visit and she kisses you on the cheek, that'll be thanks enough for me!"

A guy calls the fire department and says, "Get out here right away. My barn's on fire!" The fireman says, "How do we get there?" The guy says, "Don't you still have those little red trucks?"

A boy writes home to his dad and says, "I was going to send that ten dollars I owe you, but I already licked and sealed the envelope before I thought of it!"

A horse walks in the bar, and the bartender says, "Why the long face?"

My wife wouldn't buy a bed from the local furniture store because of their motto.....*We stand behind every bed we sell*.

You've heard of people that don't know anything? My uncle doesn't even suspect nothing!

"You think YOU'VE been waiting a long time; I'M her husband!"

A man lived in a house between an old couple and a newlywed couple. One morning the newlywed lady was hanging her husband's underwear on the clothesline. She was singing, "Sugar in the morning, sugar in the evening, sugar at supper time......"

He looked over and the old lady was hanging out the old man's underwear on the clothesline, too. She was singing, "Precious memories, how they linger......."

4

1st guy: "What's that in your lapel?"

2nd guy: "It's a chrysanthemum."

1st guy: "It looks like a rose to me."

2nd guy: "No, it's a chrysanthemum."

1st guy: "Well, if it's a chrysanthemum, spell it for me."

2nd guy: "C-R-E-S-A-N..........C-H-E-R-A-N........

C-R-I-S-S-A-N..........By golly, I think that is a

rose!"

A boy came home with a bouquet of flowers in his
hand. His dad, thinking it was odd, asked the boy about it.
He said, "Son, where did you get the bouquet?"
The kid said, "You told me when I went to see Grandma in
the hospital to get her flowers......so when she wasn't
looking, I got'em!"

A country couple had a mule hitched to a wagon heading into town. The mule stumbled and almost fell down. The man said, "That's one." A little farther down the road the mule stumbled again. The man said, "That's two." Down the road a ways, the mule stumbled again, almost falling. The man said, "That's three." He got out of the wagon, grabbed his gun, and shot the mule stone dead right there in the road.

His wife said, "You old fool. All that mule did was stumble a little! You're nothing but a stubborn old goat!"

The man looked his wife square in the eye and said, "That's one!"

I can't forget the night we were married, but Lord knows I've tried!

1st guy: "I'm going hiking in the woods."

2nd guy: "What if a snake bites you on the ankle?"

1st guy: "No problem, you take a sharp knife and make an X over the bite. Then, you have one of your friends suck the poison out, and you'll be okay."

2nd guy: "What if you sit down on an old log, and a snake bites you right where you're sitting?"

1st guy: "That's when you find out who your friends are!"

A man was telling the preacher about his financial troubles. He said, "I owe lots and lots of money. I'm just about to lose my house, my car, and everything I own!"

The preacher said, "You go home, take the Bible, open it up at random, place your finger on the page, and there you will find the answer to all of your problems."

The man did exactly what the preacher had told him to do, and sure enough, there was the answer.... Chapter 11.

Two guys were driving down the street and came upon a red traffic light. The driver didn't even slow down. He ran right through the red light.

The passenger said, "Why did you run that red light?"

The driver said, "My brother does it all the time." They came to another red light. Same thing, he ran right through it.

The passenger said, "You did it again!"

The driver said, "My brother does it all the time." A couple of blocks down the street they came to a green light, where the driver politely stopped.

The passenger asked, "What are you doing?"

The driver said, "My brother might be coming from the other way!"

A city slicker drove into a small town looking for the courthouse. Not knowing where it was, he pulled over to the curb to ask directions. A boy in a pair of bibbed overalls was leaning against a lamp post. The city slicker said, "Pardon me, Bud, can you tell me where I can find the courthouse?"

The boy said, How did you know my name was Bud?"

The city slicker said, "I guessed."

The boy said, "Then guess where the courthouse is!"

An emcee was introducing an old entertainer. He said, "He has been on stage. He has been on radio. He has been on television. In fact, he's the biggest *has been I've* ever known!"

1st guy: "I took my dad to New Orleans. He told me before we left, 'Son, if you go down to Bourbon Street, don't you go into any of those girlie shows. You might see somethin you're not supposed to see!'"

2nd guy: "Did you go in one?"

1st guy: "First one I came to!"

2nd guy: "Did you see something you weren't supposed to?"

1st guy: "I sure did!"

2nd guy: "What'd you see?"

1st guy: "I saw my daddy sitting on the very first row!"

My uncle is loaded! Filthy rich! In fact. He's got so much money he lives over the top of a bank. His *assets* over 36 million dollars.

A country boy came home from the army with a hand grenade. He had never had to use it, and always wondered if it would work. He spotted the old outhouse and decided, since the folks had indoor plumbing, they wouldn't need the old outhouse anymore.

So, he counted to three, pulled the pin, and gave the grenade a toss at the old toilet. WHAM! It blew that outhouse into a million pieces. About that time, Grandpa came out of the rubble pulling up his overalls and said, "Boy, I'm sure glad I didn't do that in the house!"

1st guy: "My wife put me on a bran diet."

2nd guy: "She did?"

1st guy: "Yeah, morning, noon, and night...bran, bran, bran."

2nd guy: "Has it kept you regular?"

1st guy: "Regular! I'm thirty days ahead!"

11

One Sunday morning, this guy woke up with laryngitis. He couldn't talk above a whisper. He knew the doctor wouldn't be in his office on Sunday, so he went to the doctor's house. He knocked on the doctor's door, and the doctor's wife answered. Whispering, he asked, "Is the doctor in?" The wife whispers back and says, "No, come on in."

Grandpa went to the doctor complaining about his ear bothering him. The doctor checked him over and found a suppository in his ear. Grandpa picked up the phone and called Grandma and said, "Don't bother looking for my hearing aid. I think I know where it's at!"

"So you're Bill's boss. My! You certainly don't LOOK like an insufferable fathead."

1st guy: "My wife is on a diet, and I'll bet she weighs herself twenty times a day. Do you know how she weighs?"

2nd guy: "No, how?"

1st guy: "Naked! The other day she embarrassed me to death she took off all her clothes and stepped up on the scales, right in front of me."

2nd guy: "Well, what's so embarrassing about that?"

1st guy: "We were right in the middle of Wal-Mart!"

My uncle invented streaking. It happened by accident one morning when he reached up to get the Preparation H and accidentally got hold of the Ben Gay instead!!"

"We are honored to have as our guest speaker, an expert on safety."

1st guy: "How's your brother?"

2nd guy: "He just got fired from the pork and bean

factory."

1st guy: "What happened?"

2nd guy: "He was putting the beans in the can upside

down, and it was giving everybody the hiccups."

George and Bill were changing clothes in the locker room after a golf game. George said, "Bill, you've got a girdle on! When did you start wearing a girdle?" Bill said, "Ever since my wife found it in the glove compartment of my car!"

My brother was the teacher's pet. I know he was, because she kept him in a cage in the back of the class!

If you eat dinner in a dinner jacket and smoke in a smoking jacket, what do you do in a windbreaker?

My wife told me to put on a clean pair of socks every day. I tried that, but after about seven days, I could hardly get my shoes on!

Two boys walking by a nudist colony decided they would have a peek inside. One boy said, "Climb up on my shoulders and look over the fence and see what's there." So, the other boy stood on his shoulders and looked over the fence.

"See anything?"

"Yeah, I see a lot of people."

"Well, are they boys or girls?"

"I can't tell! They ain't got no clothes on!"

1st guy:	"I bought a thermos bottle."
2nd guy:	"What does it do?"
1st guy:	"It keeps hot things hot and cold things cold."
2nd guy:	"What have you got in it?"
1st guy:	"Two cups of coffee and a Popsicle."

Two astronauts were in a space capsule, circling the earth. One of the astronauts went out for a space walk. After a while, when he had completed his walk, he knocked on the capsule door. The astronaut inside said, "Who is it?

My home town is so small.....we only have two yellow pages!

Glen and his wife Virginia were driving down the road when a highway patrolman pulled them over for speeding. The patrolman said, "You were speeding!"

Glen said, "I was not speeding!"

"Yes, you were," said the patrolman. "You were speeding."

Glen replied, "I was not speeding."

The patrolman asked, "Is this your wife with you?"

"Yes, it is," replied Glen.

The patrolman said, "Just tell the truth, lady, was your husband speeding or not?"

She said, "I learned a long time ago not to argue with him when he's been drinking."

———••┄┄••———

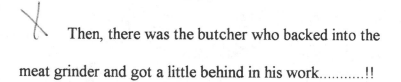 Then, there was the butcher who backed into the meat grinder and got a little behind in his work...........!!

There's a new cigarette on the market that has a little pill in the filter. You still get lung cancer, but you don't care.

A man had purchased a grandfather clock at an antique store and was carrying it down the sidewalk to put it in his pickup truck. A drunk came stumbling out of a bar, knocked the man down, and broke the clock into a million pieces.

The man said to the drunk, "Why don't you watch where you're going?"

The drunk said, "Why don't you wear a wrist watch like everyone else!"

Two boys walking along the river came upon two ladies skinny dipping. One lady felt along the bottom of the river with her foot and found an old wash tub. She picked up the tub, covered herself with it, and as mad as a hornet, came marching up the bank. She said to the boys, "Do you know what I think?....DO YOU KNOW WHAT I THINK?"

One of the boys said, "Yeah, I know what you think. You think there's a bottom in that old tub!"

A man went to the doctor and said, "Doc, I'm not feeling too good. I need a check-up."

The doctor checked him over and found a green bean in one ear, a piece of cauliflower in the other ear, and a carrot in his nose. After the exam, the doctor said to the man, "I can tell you what's wrong with you........You're not eating right!"

A preacher wrote on the information board in front of the church, *If you're tired of sin, come on in.*

The next day, he came to church and someone had written on the board with red lipstick, *But if you're not, call 555-2626!*

Then, there was the guy who sat for three hours in a car wash. He thought it was raining too hard to drive..........!!

A couple who was expecting a baby lived in the middle of Wyoming, thirty miles from town. One afternoon the wife said to her husband, "It's time!"

The guy picked up the phone and called his neighbor and said, "Get over here right away! Help me get some rags, soap, and hot water!"

The neighbor asked, "Is she gonna have the baby there?"

The guy said, "Naw, we're gonna wash the pickup truck so we can take her to the hospital."

Grandpa was filling out a credit application. One of the questions was————*Nearest relative?*

Grandpa wrote down,

twelve miles.

A honeymoon couple picked up a man's suitcase by mistake and took it to their room. The man went up to their room, and just before knocking, overheard the couple talking inside.

He said, "Whose little nose is that?"

She said, "It's yours, honey."

He said, "Whose little mouth is that?"

She said, "It's yours, honey."

He said, "Whose little eyes are those?"

She said, "They're yours, honey."

The man hollered through the door and said, "When you get to that little suitcase, that's mine!"

I was so poor when I was a kid, my neighbors had me!

A man was driving down a country road in his car and ran out of gas. He walked to a farmhouse and asked a farmer if he could borrow some gas. The farmer told him he could, but he didn't have anything to put it in but a bedpan. The guy said that would be fine and headed back to his car with the gas. He was pouring it into his car out of the bedpan when a drunk came along. The drunk took one look and said, "Boy, I didn't know that would work! I've been paying a dollar twenty-nine a gallon!"

1st guy: "My wife just bought one of those thigh masters they were advertising on TV"

2nd guy: "Has she lost any weight?"

1st guy: "No, but she can crack a walnut with her knees!"

A man answers the telephone in the middle of the night, and his wife overhears him say, "Well, how do I know? That's a thousand miles from here!" When he hung up, his wife asked, "Who was that?"

The man replied, "It was someone wanting the Coast Guard."

She said, "The Coast Guard??"

He said, "I guess they were wanting the Coast Guard. They wanted to know if the coast was clear!"

1st guy: "I got a new goat."

2nd guy: "A new goat, huh? Where do you keep it?"

1st guy: "I keep it in the house."

2nd guy: "Well, what about the smell?"

1st guy: "He'll just have to get used to it! I did!"

Wayne

1st guy: "You're a little bowlegged. Did you get that from

 ridin' a horse?"

2nd guy: "No, I got that from wearing a diaper 'til I was 21

 years old!"

Cars are so small now! I started across the road
today and one of those little cars knocked me down. Before
I could get up, another one ran up my britches leg.........I'm
sure glad he didn't make a left turn!

It was *so* cold, I saw a dog frozen to a fire hydrant.

1st guy: "Where are you from?"

2nd guy: "Burnt Mattress, Arkansas"

1st guy: "Never heard of it. Where is it located?"

2nd guy: "Just a little bit above Hot Springs."

1st guy: "I just about got killed yesterday!"

2nd guy: "What happened?"

1st guy: "Well, I was ridin' this horse when the saddle
slipped and went underneath him. He was runnin'
and buckin' and snortin' and just about kicked me
to death!"

2nd guy: "How'd you get off of him?"

1st guy: "The manager of Wal-Mart came out and
unplugged it!"

The motel manager called Grandma in room 206 and said, "You need to come and get Grandpa. He just went *number one* in the swimming pool!"

Grandma said, "How do you know it was Grandpa? There are a lot of people in the pool."

The manager said, "He was standing on the diving board when he did it!"

Two guys were in a restaurant. One guy told the waitress, "I'll have a beef tongue sandwich."

The other guy said, "How can you eat anything that's been in some animal's mouth?"

The first guy said, "Hey, you ordered eggs and I didn't say anything!"

The postmaster was giving a third grade class a tour of the post office. One kid asked, "What are those pictures on the bulletin board?"

The postmaster said, "Those are bad people. They are the ten most wanted people in America."

The kid said, "Well, why didn't they just keep'em when they took their pictures?"

A man from the church was singing a few songs to the old folks in a nursing home. When he finished, he walked up to an old man sitting in a rocking chair, who was in pretty bad shape and said, "Well, I hope you get better."

The old man said, "Well, I hope you do, too!"

A husband and wife were having a battle of the sexes when she said, "If it wasn't for the women, who would sew the buttons on your pants?"

He said, "If it wasn't for the women, we wouldn't have to wear any pants!"

1st guy: "My brother goes to college."

2nd guy: "What's he studying?"

1st guy: "He ain't studying nothin'. They're studying him!"

I knew a man who lived in Kansas. He said it was so flat out there, his dog ran off, and he could still see him for two and a half days!

The motel manager knocked on a guy's door and asked if he had a woman in the room. The man said, "No, I haven't got a woman in the room!" So the manager opened the door and threw one in.

A group of hillbillies decided to stage a march on Washington, D.C. in protest of all the hillbilly jokes. They marched from Arlington, VA to the White House, and at last report they were 15 miles south of Phoenix.

A guy walked up to his neighbor who had a dog under each arm. The guy asked, "What are you doing with these dogs?"

The neighbor said, "I got them for my wife."

The guy said,"I think you made a pretty good trade!"

A guy was telling his friend about his honeymoon in New York City. He said, "Our marriage didn't get off to a very good start. We had a big fight, and my new bride threw my coat off the Empire State Building."

The friend said, "What's so bad about that?"

He said, "I was wearing it at the time!"

Two guys were walking by a casket. One guy said to the other, "He looks good, doesn't he?"

The other guy said, "Well, he should! He just got out of the hospital."

I was in the fifth grade for five years.....I didn't want to pass Dad.

The only way I got out of school..............I married the teacher.

A man riding on a train went to the restroom to wash his face. Just as he started washing, the train rounded a curve and went into a pitch-black tunnel. His face slipped out of his hands and into the guy's hands next to him. He said to the man, "Excuse me, but that's my face you're washing."

The other guy said, "Well, if that's your face, then somebody must be washing mine."

A third guy said, "Well it ain't my face. The face I'm washing has been talking, and I haven't said a word for five minutes!"

A midget lady went to the doctor with a rash, high on her thighs. The doctor told her to lie on the table, and he would take a look.

The doctor lifted her little dress, took a pair of scissors and snipped around, then said, "Hop down, and see if that's better."

She did and said, "Doc, that's wonderful. What did you do?"

The doctor said, "I just cut a couple of inches off the top of your over shoes."

A man recorded a song in his basement..........It was a big cellar.

A little girl was being naughty, so her mom gave her a couple of swats across the bottom and sent her to her room.

The little girl backed up to a mirror, looked at her behind, and hollered, "Mama, I hope you're happy! You cracked it!"

———•••——•••———

A cowboy ran into the passenger car of a train, pulled out a gun, and said, "I'm Jesse James. I'm gonna rob all the men and kiss all the women."

A man jumped up and said, "Oh, no you're not!" His wife grabbed him by the arm and said, "You sit down and let Jesse rob this train if he wants to!"

An old farm couple, who had never seen a motorcycle, was sitting on the front porch when a motorcycle came roaring up the road.

Ma asked, "Pa, what is that?"

Pa said, "I don't know!"

He went in the house, grabbed his shotgun, and POW, shot the motorcycle all to pieces. He said, "I'm not sure what it was, but I made it turn loose of that man!"

1st guy: " Hey, I wrote a song! Here's how it goes…"

    I went down to the creek.

    I laid my clothes in the grass.

    I jumped in the water,

        Plumb up to my ……..KNEE!

2nd guy: "Well, that didn't even rhyme!"

1st guy: "It would have if the water'd been a little deeper!"

The doctor told the drunk, "You need to quit drinking, or it's going to kill you."

The drunk said, "Doc, there's a lot more old drunks than there are old doctors!"

A man running late for his cruise was rushing down the dock towards the ship. He noticed the ship was already about eight feet from the dock. He didn't want to miss his cruise, so with his luggage, he ran as hard as he could and jumped the eight feet and landed on the deck of the cruise ship.

The captain was standing there when the man landed and said, "You sir, are an idiot!"

The guy said, "I made the cruise though, didn't I?"

The captain said, "Yes, but we were just now pulling *in* to the dock!"

A boy asks a lady if she has any work for him to do. She says, "Yes, you can paint my porch." And she hands a bucket of green paint.

An hour later, he goes to the door and says, "I got it painted. And by the way lady, that's not a Porsche. That's a Corvette!"

My grandpa put his false teeth in backwards and almost chewed the back of his head off!

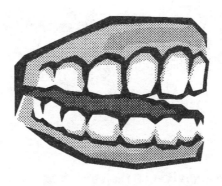

"Mr. Harkworth . . . I haven't even told the joke yet."

A guy was visiting his grandmother when he noticed a bowl of peanuts on the coffee table. He helped himself to a handful, and before long, he had eaten the whole bowl of nuts. He said to his grandmother, "Grandma, I'm sorry I ate up all of your peanuts."

She said, "That's okay, Sonny. Ever since I lost my teeth, all I can do is suck the chocolate off of them."

1st guy: "I let my brother name my twins."

2nd guy: "What did he name the girl?"

1st guy: "Denise"

2nd guy: "That's cute. What did he name the boy?"

1st guy: "Denephew!"

A man was telling his doctor about his terrible headaches. The doctor said, "When I get a bad headache, I go home and give my wife lots of hugs and kisses. That works for me. You should try it!"

Three days later the man called the doctor and said, "Doc, you were right! My headache is completely gone. And by the way, Doc, you've got a nice house!"

1st guy: "I want to ask you something. Were you in
          Springfield last Saturday night?"

2nd guy: "If I was, I can tell you. I keep everything down
          in a book. I keep in alphabetical order all my
          appointments, meetings, and activities."

1st guy: "Well, look in your book and tell me if you were
          in Springfield last Saturday night."

2nd guy: That would be found under "P" for places......

          ....Sure was! I was in Springfield last Saturday
          night!"

1st guy: "Did you meet a girl named Joyce?"

2nd guy: "That comes under "C" for contacts..............Yep,
          I met a girl named Joyce!"

1st guy: "Did you take her out to dinner?"

2nd guy   "That would be under "X" for expenses.........
          Sure did! I took her out to dinner!"

1st guy: "After dinner, did you drive her home?"

2nd guy: "That would be under "M" for mileage........I did!
           I drove her home."

1st guy: "When you got her home, did you walk her to the
           door?"

2nd guy: "That comes under "P" for pleasure........Yes, I
           did! I walked her to the door."

1st guy: "Did you kiss her good night?"

2nd guy: "That would be under "AP" for added
           pleasure........Sure did!   I kissed her good night!"

1st guy: "Look, Joyce happens to be my sister, and I didn't
           like it!"

2nd guy: "That would be under "O" for opinion.......Hey,
           look here! I didn't like it much either!"

A country boy had killed a chicken for Sunday dinner and was picking the feathers off, when he got a bright idea. He thought to himself, I'll get my electric razor and shave those little pin feathers off and save some time. He did, and it worked great.

He sent his idea in a letter to the Schick Razor Company, and they liked the idea, too. They sent him a letter back saying from now on they were going to make three kinds of razors : *men's* Schicks, *ladies'* Schicks, and *chicken's* Schicks.

The emcee said, "I'd like to tell some jokes that are so funny they would make your hair fall out, but I see a lot of you guys have already heard them."

At the cash register, a man was paying his check for a grilled cheese sandwich and a cup of soup. The waitress said, "That will be $12.95."

The man said, "$12.95! That's awfully high, isn't it?"

She said, "That's our regular price."

The man paid the check and asked the waitress, "By the way, what's that around your neck?"

She said, "That's a necklace. Why do you ask?"

The man said, "I thought it might be your garter. Everything else is so high in here!"

Two drunks were walkin' down the railroad track. One said to the other, "I don't mind these short steps, but these low handrails are killing me!"

Two guys were hunting in the woods and came upon a big hole in the ground. They threw a little rock in it, but they never did hear it hit the bottom. They picked up a big rock and dropped it in the hole. They never heard it hit the bottom, either. Determined to find out how deep the hole was, they picked up a railroad tie and threw it in the hole. Just as they threw the railroad tie in the hole, a black and white goat ran by them at about a hundred miles an hour and jumped in the hole. The guys scratched their heads and thought that was the strangest thing they had ever seen. They looked up and saw a man walking towards them.

The man said, "Y'all haven't seen a black and white goat, have you?"

One guy said, "Yeah! A black and white goat just jumped down this hole!"

The man said, "Well, that couldn't have been my goat. My goat was tied to a railroad tie!"

A man goes in an appliance shop and tells the clerk, "I've gotta get a bigger TV set!"

The clerk asked, "Is yours too small?"

The man said, "Yes, it's too small! When I watch Matt Dillon and Chester, I can only see one of them! When I watch Andy and Barney, I can only see one of them! When I watch Roy Rogers and Dale Evans, I can only see one of them! The other night, Dolly Parton was on there................I've gotta get a bigger television!"

A wife called her husband at work and said, "Honey, come home as fast as you can. There are about fifteen dogs in our yard!"

He said, "Are they mad?"

She said, "Well, two of them ain't!"

The teacher asked the boy why he was so sleepy. The boy said, "Well, last night Pa heard something in the chicken house, so he grabbed the shotgun and crept down by the chicken house to see what it was. All he was wearing was his long-handled underwear with the back flap down. Just as he stuck the gun in the chicken house, our old huntin' dog cold-nosed Pa...........and we've been picking chickens all night long!"

Why did the guy bury his horse on a hillside?

Because he was dead.........!

A drunk and a dog were standing on a street corner. A guy walked up and asked the drunk, "Does your dog bite?"

The drunk said, "Heck, no!"

The guy reached out to pet the dog and Grrrrrrrrrrrr! The dog took half his arm off. He said, "I thought you said your dog didn't bite!"

The drunk said, "Heck, that ain't *my* dog!"

A tongue-tied weather man said, ".....and tonight there's a good chance for schattered scowers......."

A farmer went to the hen house one morning to gather the eggs. He reached under the chicken for an egg, but there was no egg. There was a nickel. He thought this was strange, but went on with his work. The next morning he went to gather the eggs.....No egg! There was a dime. The farmer was really puzzled now. The third morning he went to gather the eggs.........no egg! There was a quarter. The farmer called the veterinarian and said, "There's something wrong with my hen! The first morning there was no egg, but there was a nickel. The second morning there was no egg, but there was a dime. The third morning there was no egg, but there was a quarter!"

The veterinarian said, "There's nothing wrong with your hen. She's just going through the change!"

Grandpa put on a life jacket and jumped into the motel swimming pool. When he hit the water, he lost his swimming trunks and the life jacket had him upside down with his bottom sticking out of the water.

A lady was standing there and saw Grandpa's bare bottom and screamed, "Help, quick! Somebody call 911! This poor man has split his head wide open!"

An old country boy was driving in New York City where traffic was bumper to bumper. He said, "Traffic was so close, he pushed in his cigarette lighter and the lady in the car in front of him yelled, "OUCH!"

My neighbor got in trouble today. His wife told him to drop his pants at the cleaners...........and he did!

A boy from the Ozarks took his first train ride through the mountains. Along the way, the conductor was passing out fruit for the passengers to snack on. The boy had never eaten a banana before, so he picked out a banana from the front of the basket and peeled it back. Just as he took a bite, the train went into a tunnel where it was pitch black. When the train came out of the tunnel into the sunlight, the conductor asked the boy if he would like another banana.

The boy said, "No way! I took one bite of that last banana and went stone blind!"

I wanted to come to St. Louis in the worst way, and that's just how I came. The worst way.......right through East St. Louis!"

1st guy: "I wrecked my car."

2nd guy: "What happened?"

1st guy: "Well, I was driving down the road. I looked up, and the first thing I saw was a bull coming out of an alfalfa field."

2nd guy: "What was the second thing you saw?"

1st guy: "Alfalfa coming out of the bull."

My uncle is in the meat-packing business.........He makes women's girdles!

 After finishing a jigsaw puzzle, the man told his neighbor, "I finished it in just three weeks!"

The neighbor said, "That's pretty good!"

The man said, "You darn right it is! The box said two to four years!"

I've loved the same woman for thirty years........and if my wife ever finds out about it, she'll kill me!

My brother was so ugly, when he was a boy, my folks had to tie a pork chop around his neck so the dog would play with him!

Grandpa walked into the doctor's office and there was a dollar bill on the wall behind the desk. Grandpa asked, "What's that dollar bill?"

The nurse said, "That's the first dollar the doctor ever earned."

She took Grandpa back to an examination room, where he noticed a skeleton in the corner. Grandpa said, "That's nice. He kept his first patient, too."

A little boy was sitting on the school house steps smoking a cigarette. The preacher walked by and saw the boy smoking and said to the boy, "Do you know where boys like you go when they smoke?"

The kid said, "Yeah, most of them go out behind the bus barn."

The farmer's bull wasn't paying any attention to the cows, which concerned the farmer. He called the veterinarian and told him his problem. The vet said, "Come by the office. I have some pills that will help your bull."

The farmer picked up the pills and gave some to the bull, and in no time at all the bull was chasing every cow in the pasture.

A neighbor heard about the farmer's bull and the pills and the results. He asked the farmer, "What kind of pills are they?"

The farmer said, "I don't know what kind they are, but they taste a little like peppermint."

1st guy: "I come from Buffalo."

2nd guy: "Oh really! I just come from ordinary parents!

Two kids were talking. One kid said, "I'm gonna be an astronaut when I grow up! I'm gonna be the first person on the sun!"

The other boy said, "You can't go to the sun! It's hot on the sun!"

The first kid said, "Well, I'll just go at night!"

After two years of being divorced, an old couple got remarried. What happened was, the old man owed her a lot of alimony. He got way behind on his payments, so she repossessed him.

A politician was giving a speech to a group of Indians on the reservation. Over the P.A. system he would shout, "I'll see to it that you get better roads." At that remark, all the Indians would yell, "Hanzanga!"

He shouted louder, "I'll get you better jobs." Again, all of the Indians yelled, "Hanzanga!" "I'll have you living in better houses," he claimed. "Hanzanga!" yelled the Indians.

The politician thought he had made a great speech and really had the Indians on his side.

The chief asked the politician to tour one of the farms in the community before going back to the city. As they walked through the barnyard where the farmer kept his bulls, the chief turned to the politician and said, "Be careful! Don't step in the hanzanga."

Two guys were talking when one guy says, "You sure have a good lookin' sister. But tell me, where did she get those big hands?"

The other guy says, "Well, when we were kids we played in the snow a lot.   Playing in the snow makes your hands big."

The first guy says, "Where did she get those big feet?"

The other guy says, "Same reason. Playing in the snow makes your feet big."

The first guy says, "Well, she sure must have *sat* in the snow a lot!"

A man and wife wanted to take a helicopter ride, but it was too expensive. The pilot said, "I'll tell you what I'll do. I'll let you both ride for free if you promise not to yell or scream. If you scream, I'll have to charge you double!"

The couple agreed to his terms, and off they went for their ride. The pilot tried his best to scare them. He did all kinds of spins and loops and swirls, but they never screamed once.

When they finally landed, the man said, "I never screamed once, but I almost did!"

The pilot said, "When was that?"

The man said, "When my wife fell out of the helicopter!"

A man was sitting in the waiting room at the doctor's office, when all of a sudden, the office door flew open. An old lady in her '80's ran out of the office, jumped over the coffee table, and ran out the front door into the street.

The man waiting asked the doctor, "What in the world is wrong with that old lady?"

The doctor said, "Nothing, I just told her she was going to have a baby."

The man said, "That old lady is gonna have a baby!?!"

The doctor said, "No, she's not really going to have a baby, but I sure did cure her hiccups!"

The father said, "I spent forty thousand dollars sending my son to college so he could play football, and all I got was a *quarter*back!"

A drunk walks into a bar and asks the bartender, "Do you know me?"

The bartender says, "I don't believe I do."

The drunk says, " Have you ever talked to me before?"

The bartender says, "I don't think so."

The drunk says, "Well, then how do you know it's me?"

A guy riding on a train had to use the restroom. Suddenly, he reached up and started pulling on the emergency cord. The train screeched to a halt, throwing everyone out of their seats. Luggage went everywhere. The conductor asked the man, "Buddy, why'd you stop the train?"

The guy said, "I've got hemorrhoids."

The conductor said, "Heck, a lot of people have hemorrhoids!

The guy said, "Wrapped around an axle?"

I'm a Baptist. And one thing about us Baptists......when we go to heaven, we always have to take a covered dish!

Two guys were talking. One said to the other, "Do you remember years ago when we were traveling and our car broke down, and we spent the night with that widow woman in that pretty farm house?"

The other guy said, "Yes, I remember that."

The first guy said, "And, do you remember, you stayed in the house with the widow woman and made me sleep out in the barn?"

The other guy said, "Yes. I remember that, too."

He said, "Tell me, did you give her *my* name? Did you tell her you were *me*?"

The guy said, "I sure did. I remember doing that."

He said, "That's just what I thought. I got a letter from her lawyer. She died last month and left me her farm."

1st guy: "Do you believe in the two-party system

2nd guy: "Sure do! One on Friday and one on

       Saturday!"

A Texan was bragging about how big his ranch was.
He said, "My ranch is *so* big, I can get on my horse and
ride a half a day and still never get to the other side of it."

An old boy standing there said, "You know, I had a
horse just like that one time!"

Do you know what the snail said when he was riding
on the back of a turtle????

"Wheeeeeeeeeeeeeeeeeeeeeeeeeeeeeeeeeeeeeeeeeee!"

A man calls the doctor and says, "Doc, I've broken my arm in three places. What should I do?"

The doctor says, "Stay out of those places."

"You're in the wrong line — the cashier is this way."

1st guy: "I caught a twelve pound bass."

2nd guy: "Where'd you catch him?"

1st guy: "Right there in the lip."

Six elephants in the big top circus were hooked up,
trunk-to-tail, going around in the circus ring. One elephant
tripped and fell down and pulled the tail out of five
elephants.

1st guy: "How was the carnival?

2nd guy: "Fair."

A polar bear and his son were sitting on an iceberg when the son asked his dad, "Dad, do we have any grizzly bears in our family?"

His dad said, "No, son, we're just polar bears."

He said, "Do we have any brown bears in our family?"

His dad said, "No, we're just polar bears."

The son said, "Well, Dad, do we have any panda bears in our family."

His dad said, "No, we're just polar bears. Why do you ask?"

The son said, "I don't know about you, Dad, but I'm getting pretty cold."

Three Texans were talking. One said, "I own 6,450 acres. I call mine the Rockin' "R" Ranch." The second Texan said, "I own 7,500 acres. I call mine the Flyin' "W" Ranch." The third Texan said, "I only have 15 acres." The other two laughed and said, "What do you call yours?" He said, "**Downtown Dallas**."

A man was walking down the road pulling a log chain, when a guy asked, "What are you doing pulling that chain?"

The man said, "Did you ever see anybody try to push one?"

The circus came to a small country town. One of the elephants got loose and got in a lady's garden. She called the sheriff's department and said, "There's a big critter in my garden, and I don't know quite what it is."

The sheriff asked, "What is it doing?"

The lady said, "It's pulling up my turnips with its tail."

The sheriff asked, "What's it doing with the turnips?"

She said, "You wouldn't believe me if I told you."

1st Guy: "I married a twin."

2nd Guy: "How can you tell them apart?"

1st Guy: "It's easy. Her brother is a lot taller."

A man fell asleep sitting on the front pew of the church. The preacher was preaching hell, fire, and brimstone and said, "If there's anyone here today who wants to go to Hell, STAND UP."

The man heard, STAND UP and jumped to his feet. He looked at the preacher and said, "Preacher, I don't know what we're voting on, but it looks like you and me are the only ones for it."

A man goes into a ladies' clothing store to purchase a new bra for his wife. The clerk asks, "What size?"

The man says, "7 1/2".

The clerk says, "7 1/2--How did you measure that?"

The man said, "With my hat."

The teacher asked a little boy in school, "Who signed the Declaration of Independence?"

The boy said, "I don't know, and I don't give a darn."

The teacher called the boy's dad down to school and told him what the boy had said. She asked the dad, "What do you think we should do about that?"

The dad turned to his son and said, "Boy, if you signed that darn thing, you'd better fess up to it."

A country boy was standing in line to get an army physical when the doctor grabbed him and told him to turn his head and cough.

The boy said, "Doc, I've heard of low colds, but this is ridiculous."

A man was fishing and came upon a boat that had capsized with several guys in it. He would grab them one by one, by the hair of the head and drag them into his boat. All of a sudden, a bald headed man came bobbin' out of the water. The man hit him on the top of the head with a boat paddle and said, "You go down and come up head first next time."

An Indian in Arizona was sending smoke signals by waving a blanket over a campfire. He didn't realize that just across the border in Nevada, the army had set off an atomic bomb at a bomb test site. The Indian stood and watched a big mushroom cloud billow up and said, "Darn, I wish I'd said that!"

Grandpa came to visit and had to sleep with his grandson. Before going to sleep, the little boy crawled out of bed and kneeled down beside the bed.

Grandpa thought, how nice, the boy is saying his prayers. Maybe I ought to say mine, too. So, Grandpa got out of bed and kneeled down on the other side of the bed.

The grandson looked over at Grandpa and said, "Boy, is Momma ever gonna' be mad at you! The pot's on *this* side of the bed!"

1st guy: "My wife has been on a new banana diet."

2nd guy: "Has she lost any weight?"

1st guy: "No, but you should see her climb trees!"

A doctor examined a man in the hospital and said, "I've got good news and bad news."

The man said, "Give me the bad news first."

The doctor said, "We're gonna have to amputate both legs."

The man said, "What good news could there possibly be?"

The doctor said, "I think I've got your shoes sold."

1st Guy: "The candle factory I work at burned down last night."

2nd Guy: "What did you do?"

1st Guy: "Everyone just stood around and sang Happy Birthday."

I knew a girl who had a dress made entirely out of chicken feathers-----The men watched her like a hawk.

A lady was taking a bath when her little boy ran into the bathroom and said, "Mama, there's a blind man at the door."

"A blind man?", she asked.

The kid said, "Yeah, there's some blind guy on the front porch."

Without bothering to put on clothes, she ran to the door and threw it open. Some strange man was standing there and said, "What do you want me to do with these venetian blinds?"

Two old country boys were talking.

1st Guy: "What did you get your wife for Christmas?"

2nd Guy: "I bought her seven pairs of underwear."

1st Guy: "Seven pairs of underwear?"

2nd Guy: "Yeah, they were embroidered on each

leg.......Monday, Tuesday, Wednesday,

Thursday, Friday, Saturday, Sunday.

1st Guy: "What did she get you for Christmas?"

2nd Guy: "She bought me twelve pairs."

1st Guy: "Twelve pairs of underwear? How come so

many?"

2nd Guy: "Well----------January, February, March, April,

Ma........."

1st guy: "If you had ten dollars in your left pocket and ten dollars in your right   pocket, do you know what you would have?"

2nd guy: "Yeah, I know what I would have. I'd have somebody else's pants on!"

A man was staying in a motel when the maid knocked on the door. She said, "Can I come in and clean up?"

He said, "Sure, I don't care!" So she came in and took a shower.

1st guy: "You don't know anything about farms or farm

life. I'll bet you wouldn't know a goose from a

gander."

2nd guy: "Well, back home where I'm from, we don't

worry about that. We just throw'em in a pen and

let'em figure it out for themselves!"

1st guy: "I have a PHD."

2nd guy: "You have a doctorate degree?"

1st guy: "No! I have a P-H-D, ...a post-

hole digger!"

1st guy: "I saw you ridin' a horse one time, and you were ridin' him backwards."

2nd guy: "Well, you don't know which way I was going, now do you?"

"I can't give you a raise . . . however I can invite you to dinner, once or twice a month."

Daddy took his little boy to a crowded mall. Right in the middle of the mall, the little boy yelled at the top of his voice, "Daddy! I need to go to the bathroom!"

He promptly pulled the boy aside and told him never to do that again. He said, "If you need to go to the bathroom, just say you need to <u>whisper</u>, and I'll know what you want."

Later that night, Daddy was half asleep on the couch when his little boy came running in and said, "Daddy, I need to <u>whisper</u>."

Daddy said, "Well, just whisper in my ear, son."

1st guy: "My dog had fifty puppies."

2nd guy: "What kind of dog is it?"

1st guy: "Female."

1st guy: "Do you like Westerns on television?"

2nd guy: "Shoot, I've watched so many westerns on TV,

my TV's bowlegged!"

Grandma went to the doctor, and after her check up the doctor said, "I've got some good news for you. You're gonna have a baby."

Grandma went straight to the phone and called Grandpa. She said, "I've told you and told you to be careful. Now look what you've done! You've gone and got me pregnant!"

Grandpa said, "Who is this?"

On a trip to South America, a man finds a parrot that could speak six different languages. He thought his mother would like something nice from South America, so he bought the bird and mailed it home to her. A week later, he called his mother and said, "Mom, how did you like the bird?"

She said, "It was delicious!"

He said, "Mom, you weren't supposed to eat that bird! It could speak six different languages!"

She said, "Well, it should have said something!"

You can lead a horse to water.....................but if you can get him to float on his back, you've done something!

A man went out to California to see Roy Rogers and Dale Evans. Roy was busy in the barn, so the man was talking to Dale. "Dale," he said, "I'd like to see that famous horse of Roy's, Trigger."

Dale said, "Oh, Trigger is dead, but Roy had him stuffed."

He said, "Well, I'd sure like to see that famous dog, Bullet."

Dale said, "Bullet is dead, too, but Roy had him stuffed."

He said, "I'll bet you hope Roy goes before you do!"

John Deere has a new slogan - -*We stand behind everything we sell, except our manure spreaders.*

A man went to the doctor to get fitted for a new glass eye. He asked the doctor how he should clean it.

The doctor told him he could buy an expensive lubricant or just use plain old saliva. The man said, "Heck, I'll just use saliva!"

The next day, the man was cleaning his eye and swallowed it. He went back to the doctor and told him what had happened. The doctor had the man get on his hands and knees on the examining table, and with a scope the doctor was looking up the opposite end, trying to locate the glass eye.

The man peeked around at the doctor and asked, "Do you see anything?"

The doctor said, "Not yet!"

The man said, "That's funny. I can see you!"

The drunk said, "I don't drink much anymore. I've got to where I spill most of it."

My wife is a Dolly Parton, Barbara Mandrell, and Tanya Tucker all rolled into one......................She'll weigh about 400 pounds!

1st guy: "How's your son?"

2nd guy: "He's walkin' and talkin' now. He's at that cute stage, saying 'Mama' and 'Dada'. He turned his cereal bowl over on top of his head this morning and said, 'Snap, crackle, pop'!"

1st guy: "How old is he now?"

2nd guy: "He's seventeen!"

1st guy: "I named my farm Oleo Acres."

2nd guy: "Why did you name it that?"

1st guy: "It's a cheap spread."

Whiskey and women killed my Grandpa..............He couldn't get either one, so he just lay down and died.

A guy was painting a yellow stripe down the middle of the highway with a brush and a bucket of paint. The first day, he painted two miles of stripe. The second day, he painted three hundred yards. The third day, he only painted ten feet of stripes. The boss asked him why he only painted ten feet that day. The guy said, "Shoot, Boss, it's a long way back to the bucket!"

Two guys were out squirrel hunting. One of them stuttered, and the other had the shakes. They spotted a squirrel in a tree. The one who stuttered pulled up and shot and missed. The other guy with the shakes pulled up and BANG! The squirrel dropped to the ground.

The stuttering guy said, "W-w-w-ell, you should h-h-have s-s-s-s-shot him. You a-a-aimed all over the t-t-t-tree!"

A guy painting his mailbox in the middle of July just about has a heat stroke, because the directions on the paint can said, **"Put on two coats."**

John and Bill were going to a Halloween party dressed as a bull. John was in the front of the bull suit, and Bill was in the back. They were taking a short cut through a field when Bill said to John, "There's a bull coming straight for us. What are we going to do?"

John said, "I'm gonna stop and graze. I suggest you brace yourself!"

A man approaches an old lady in a nursing home and asks, "Do you know who I am?"

The old lady says, "No, but if you'll go up to the front desk, they'll tell you who you are!"

A guy calls the front desk in the hotel and says, "Hey, I've gotta leak in my sink!"

The desk clerk says, "Well, go ahead. Everybody else does!"

Two ladies were marching in the Salvation Army band in the 4th of July parade. After the parade, they were taking a shower at the local high school girls' locker room.

One lady looked over and said, "Martha, you've got the biggest belly button I've ever seen on a person!"

Martha said, "Oh, yeah, you laugh! Next year in the parade, you can carry the flag, and I'll play the drum!"

My luck is *so* bad, I bought a suit with two pairs of pants.................and burned a hole in the *coat*.

Two guys were riding on an airplane, when one says, "I think I'm gonna throw up!"

The other guy says, "Just grab that air sick bag in front of you!"

The first guy says, "I would, but I'm afraid she'll slap me silly!"

My luck is *so* bad, I could be in a room full of black widow spiders and stomp on my own toe.

John Deere has a new tractor. It doesn't have a seat or a steering wheel. It's for farmers who have lost their rears and don't know which way to turn.

A newsman asked the farmer what he was going to do with the eight million dollars he had won in the state lottery.

The farmer said, "I guess I'll just keep on farmin' 'til it's all gone."

Two rabbits were running across the field with six dogs chasing them. One rabbit said to the other, "Let's stop and out number them."

The other rabbit said, "We'd better keep running. I'm your brother."

A little boy says to his mom, "Mom, we can throw our trash out of the car now. We just passed a sign that said, 'Fine for Littering'."

A man went to the front desk at the hotel and demanded a refund. He said, "I didn't sleep a wink last night!"

The desk clerk asked, "What was the problem?"

He said, "The couple in the room next to me ate candy bars all night long!"

"Candy bars?" the desk clerk said.

He said, "I guess that's what they were doing. All night long she kept saying, "Oh, Henry!"

Our local veterinarian is also the local taxidermist.
Either way you get your dog back!

My car is equipped with duel air bags,............my
wife and my mother-in-law.

Optometrist: "How's your vision?"

Patient: "Well, I think it's pretty good."

Optometrist: "Can you see very far away?"

Patient: "Well, I can see the moon. How far's

      that?

Optometrist: "Have your eyes ever been checked?"

Patient: "No, they've always been blue."

I went in a bar one time that was so rough they checked you for a gun.........and if you didn't have one, they gave you one.

I bought a watch that was waterproof, dust proof, rust proof, stainless steel back, anti-magnetic....................it caught on fire.

A man went to his mother-in-law's for dinner. There were eight people and only five pork chops. He said, "I thought it was kind of odd, but the three pork chops I had were delicious."

I know one thing. The next time I go to Hawaii where they wear all those grass skirts, I'm gonna take a Weedeater!

I washed the cats today.............................and my tongue is still sore!

"I feel guilty asking you to take so much work home with you, Harkworth. Why don't you sleep here nights?"

I took a pleasure trip last night. I took my mother-in-law to the airport.

A drunk was digging around on the sidewalk under a street light, when a policeman walked up and said, "What are you doing?"

The drunk said, "I lost my wallet."

The policeman asked, "Where did you lose it?"

The drunk said, "Back there in the alley."

The policeman said, "Then why are you looking out here?"

The drunk said, "The light's better."

A lady goes to the dentist and tells the dentist, "I'd just as soon have a baby as to have a tooth pulled!"

The dentist says, "Well, make up your mind, lady, so I'll know which way to tilt this chair!"

Grandma and Grandpa were sitting on the porch swing when Grandma said, "Grandpa, why don't you sit close to me like you used to?" So, Grandpa scooted over close to her. She said, "Grandpa, why don't you put your arm around me like you used to?" So, Grandpa put his arm around her. She said, "Grandpa, why don't you nibble on my ear like you used to?"

Grandpa got up and started to go into the house. Grandma said, "Where are you going?" Grandpa said, "I'm goin' in the house to get my teeth!

I was so poor when I was a kid, I didn't have any clothes until I was eight years old. Finally, my dad bought me a cap so I could look out the window!

The doctor told his patient, "I want you to jog five miles a day and call me in one week."

The patient called in a week. The doctor said, "How are you feeling?"

The patient said, "I feel fine, but I'm thirty miles from home."

My hometown was so small, we didn't have a town drunk. We all took turns.

Grandma and Grandpa were sitting on the porch talking. Grandpa said, "Ma, I'd like to have some ice cream."

Grandma said, "I'll go fix you some."

About thirty minutes later she came out with a plate of bacon and scrambled eggs.

Grandpa said, "Ma, you're getting so forgetful! You can't remember anything. I told you I wanted my eggs over easy!"

We finally painted a yellow stripe down the middle of Main Street.............but it just kept washing off the gravel.

Our town is so small, we don't have any heavy industry. The only heavy industry we have is an Avon lady. She weighs about four hundred and fifty pounds.

I knew a man who lied so much he couldn't even call his own dogs. They wouldn't believe him.

A dentist checks a man over and tells him, "Well, your teeth are all right, but your gums are gonna have to go!"

I knew a lady who had so many facelifts, every time she smiled she would pull her panty hose up!

A fellow took his racehorse to England for a big race. Just before the race, he reached in his pocket and gave his horse a pill. The Duke of Marlboro was standing there and saw this and said, "Hey, I saw what you did. We're going to have to disqualify your horse."

The man said, "That was nothing but a sugar pill. I'll prove it." So, he swallowed one of the pills and gave the Duke of Marlboro one. He said, "See, they're nothing but sugar pills."

That seemed to satisfy the Duke of Marlboro, so he let the horse in the race. Just before the race was about to start, the man called his jockey to the side and said, "When the gates open, you hold on tight, because there's only two things that can beat you in this race. One of them is me, and the other is the Duke of Marlboro!"

A man cut a round hole in the ice and dropped a hook and line down to do some ice fishing. A big voice boomed out, "THERE'S NO FISH UNDER THE ICE!"

The startled man hollered out, "Is that you, Lord?"

The voice boomed out again, "No, I'm the hockey rink manager! There are no fish under the ice!"

A city slicker shyster stopped at a small country service station to buy gasoline. He gave the country boy working there a counterfeit eighteen-dollar bill.

The city slicker asked, "Can you break this?"

The country boy said, "Heck yeah! How would you like it? Three sixes or two sevens and a four?"

This is the story of the three old maids. The first old maid said, "Somebody's been eating my porridge."

The second old maid said, "Somebody's been eating my porridge."

The third old maid said, "Somebody's been eating my porridge, and they ate it all up!"

They went to the living room....................

The first old maid said, "Somebody's been sitting in my chair."

The second old maid said, "Somebody's been sitting in my chair."

The third old maid said, "Somebody's been sitting in my chair, and they broke it down!"

They went to their bedrooms..................

The first old maid said, "Somebody's been sleeping

in my bed!"

The second old maid said, "Somebody's been sleeping in my bed!"

The third old maid said, with a slight chuckle in her voice, "Evenin', ladies!"

If I had known I was going to live this long, I would have taken better care of myself!

I'm getting pretty good at golf.   NOW, I can hit it about every time I throw it up!

I knew a lady who had so many facelifts, every time she smiled she would pull her panty hose up!

A country boy went to a lumberyard and said, "I'd like to buy some lumber."

The man asked, "What kind of lumber, 2 by 4's, 4 by 6's, 8 by 10"s, 6 by 8's, or what?"

The country boy said, "2 by 4's."

The man asked, "What kind? Ash, pine, walnut, birch, what?"

The boy said, "Pine."

The man asked, "How long do you want them?"

The country boy said, "I want'em a long time! I'm gonna build a barn."

Two guys came in the clubhouse after a round of golf, both soaking wet. The club pro asked, "How was your game?"

One said, "It was the worst game of golf I've ever had. On the second hole, it started pouring down rain. We all got drenched. Then, on the fourth hole, Fred, one of the guys we were playing with, had a heart attack and died. The rest of the day it was hit the ball, drag Fred, hit the ball, drag Fred!"

I checked into a motel the other day. They said I would have to make my own bed..............so they handed me a hammer and some nails.

I knew a girl so skinny...............

she could change clothes in a shotgun barrel.

———

she had to run around in the shower to get wet.

———

if she turned sideways and stuck out her tongue,

she'd look like a zipper.

———

she could drink a bottle of strawberry pop and look

like a thermometer.

———

she could step in a Coke bottle.

———

she swallowed an olive one time and four boys left

town.

A lady wanted her brother to keep her cat, Fluffy, while she went on a driving trip to California. She stopped in Kansas City and called her brother and asked about her cat. He said, "The cat's fine." She called from Denver. He said, "The cat's fine."

She called from Phoenix. He said, "The cat's dead."

She said, "Dead! Well, you could have broken the news a little easier to me about my Fluffy! You could have first said, 'Fluffy is on the roof, but the fire department is here with a ladder'. And when I called again, you could have said, 'They are trying to get her down.' When I called again, you could have told me the fireman had her, but she fell and passed away. You didn't have to say, 'The cat's dead!' Oh, and by the way, how is Mother?"

Her brother said, "Mother's on the roof!"

A guy goes into a barbershop and asks the barber, "How many before me?"

The barber says, "Eight." The guy leaves. The next day, the same thing, "How many before me?"

The barber says, "Nine." The man leaves.

The barber tells his partner, "If that guy comes in here again, follow him and see where he goes."

The next day, sure enough, he was back. So, his partner follows the man and comes back to report to the barber. The barber asks, "Well, where did he go?" The partner says, "Your house!"

A hippie was walking down the street with one shoe on. A guy walked up and said to the hippie, "What did you do, buddy, lose a shoe?"

The hippie said, "No, I found one."

A farmer forgot and left the milking machine on the cow all night long. When he got up the next morning, the cow was wrong side out!

I bought my wife one of those living bras.............................but it died. She didn't know how to feed it!

1st guy: "What did you get your wife for Christmas?"

2nd guy: "Nothing, she didn't use what I got her last year!"

1st guy: "What did you get her last year?"

2nd guy: "A cemetery plot."

A lady was heading to the grocery store, when she noticed her sink had clogged up, so she called a plumber. She waited and waited, and when the plumber didn't show, she went on to the store.

While she was gone, the plumber came and knocked on the door. The lady had a parrot inside that asked, "Who is it?"

The guy said, "It's the plumber!"

The parrot said, "Who is it?"

The guy said, "It's the plumber!"

The parrot said, "Who is it?"

The guy said, "IT'S THE PLUMBER!!!!"

The plumber was so flustered he had a heart attack and died there on the front porch. The lady came home with her groceries, saw the man lying there and asked, "My goodness, who is that?"

The parrot said, "It's the plumber."

A guy wins the eight million-dollar lottery and runs home and tells his wife, "I just won the lottery! Pack your bags!"

"Where are we going?" She asks

He said, "<u>We</u> aren't going anywhere. Pack **your** bags."

A lady wanted to carry her white poodle on the plane, but was told the dog had to ride in the cargo section. When she reached her destination, the baggage boy noticed her dog was dead.

The baggage boy called a pet store and asked if they had a white poodle. The pet store clerk said, "Yes." The baggage boy hurried over and bought the poodle, brought it back, took the little collar off her dog, put it on the new dog, and stuck it in the cage.

When the woman reached the baggage area she said, "This isn't my dog!" The baggage boy said, "Yes, this is your dog........white poodle! It's got your little collar on it!"

She said, "It is **not** my dog! My dog was dead! I was just taking it home to bury it!"

A guy called the police and said, "There's a dead man on my front porch. The policeman said, "Is he dead, or do you assume he's dead?"

The guy said, "Well, I just assume he's dead. He's been lying out there a month."

The policeman asked, "Where do you live?

The guy said, "1304 Albuquerque Lane."

The policeman inquired, "How do you spell that?"

The guy said,

"ALBEK..............ALBERK...............ALLBIK.......

.....I'm gonna have to call you back."

The policeman asked, "Why do you need to call me back?"

The guy said, "Because it's gonna take me a little while to drag him over to Elm Street."

Articles found in a country newspaper

Chain saw for sale. Only used one time. Call 555-2625. Ask for Lefty.

———

Someone shot a dog in the west end.........

———

A lady was shot and the bullet is in her yet........

———

The mayor's wife had her gall bladder removed and a new washer installed.

———

Someone stole all the commodes from the police station. They have nothing to go on.

———

A lady stabbed her husband 152 times. She said she couldn't shut off the electric knife.

Wanted: Single lady with tractor for a serious relationship. Please send a picture of the tractor.

I'm so broke I've been going down to Kentucky Fried Chicken just to lick other people's fingers.

My wife put her bra on backwards..................and it fit!

My wife is *so* ugly, when she was born the doctor slapped her mother!

Last year at Christmas, I hung a pair of my wife's stockings by the fireplace, and it made her mad. Of course, she was still wearing them at the time!

My wife is *so* ugly, tears run down the back of her neck to keep from crossing her face!

My wife looks better since she had her nose fixed. She moved it over to the middle of her face!

A lady staying in a hotel called the desk clerk and said, "There's a man in the next building with his window shades wide open, walking around stark naked."

The desk clerk went up to her room, looked out the window, and said, "Lady, I don't see any naked man."

The lady said, "Well, you stand on that dresser and take a look."

I'm not saying my wife doesn't have any teeth, but on Halloween, she's the only one who bobs for *applesauce*.

A guy driving down the road saw a sign that read: FREE PICNIC TABLES AHEAD. So, he stopped and got two of them.

An eight-year-old boy was visiting his aunt, when the aunt's boyfriend knocked on the door. She didn't want the kid to know she had a boyfriend, so she put the kid in a closet and said, "Wait in here." About that time, the aunt's husband came home, so she put the boyfriend in the closet, too.

The boyfriend and the little boy were sitting in the closet when the kid said, "Boy, it's really dark in here. I think I'm gonna scream!" The boyfriend said, "Don't scream. I'll give you five dollars not to scream."

A few minutes went by and the kid said again, "I think I'm gonna scream!"

The boyfriend said, "Don't scream. Here's another five dollars." The kid made about seventy bucks sitting in the closet. Finally, the husband left. The aunt let the boyfriend and the kid out of the closet, and they left.

Now, the kid started feeling badly about taking the

boyfriend's money, and decided he would go and confess.

He was sitting in the confessional when the priest said, "Can I help you, my son?"

The kid said, "Boy, it's really dark in here. I think I' gonna scream."

The priest said, "You ain't gonna start that again, are you?"

I went out the other day to catch a plane. Boy! They're hard to catch 'til they land.

A lady and her little boy were driving down the street with a cop right on their tails. She was afraid to look and see if the cop was trying to pull her over, so she asked the little boy to see if the policeman had his red lights on.

The kid said, "Yep, nope, yep, nope, yep, nope................."

Eight-year-old Johnny, who had never spoken a word in his life, was eating breakfast with his parents, when all of a sudden he said, "This oatmeal has lumps in it."

His mother was overjoyed and said, "Johnny, you can talk! All these years you haven't spoken a word. Why did you wait until now to speak?"

Johnny said, "Because this is the first time the oatmeal ever had lumps in it."

My Wife is so cross-eyed, she can lie on her back and look down a well!

My wife is *so* cross-eyed, one eye looks at Dallas and the other at Fort Worth

1st guy: "My uncle wrote the song, <u>The Hokey Pokey</u>."

2nd guy: "I've heard that song all my life."

1st guy: "He died last month, but they haven't been able to have a funeral."

2nd guy: "Why not?"

1st guy: "Well, he'll put his left foot in, and he'll take his left foot out..........then he'll shake it all about."

A man was lifting his arm to show the doctor and said, "Doctor, it hurts when I do that."

The doctor said, "Well, don't do that!"

Two guys were walking down the sidewalk when one said to the other, "I had a dream last night. I dreamed I went to the circus. I saw all the clowns and elephants. It was a good dream."

The other guy said, "I had a good dream last night, too. I dreamed three good looking girls came over to the house. We had a big party, just me and those three girls.

The first guy said, "Why didn't you call me?"

The other one said, "I tried to, but they said you had gone to the circus!"

The policeman asked the guy, "How come you ran over that man lying in the road." The guy said, "Heck, I thought he was dead!"

———————•᛭•———————

Grandma and Grandpa went to see a marriage counselor.

Grandma told him that Grandpa never paid attention to her anymore.

The marriage counselor came around the desk, bent Grandma over, and gave her a big kiss, right on the mouth. He said, "Now Grandpa, she needs that about twice a week."

Grandpa said, "Well, I'll try to bring her in on Tuesdays and Thursdays."

A man with a rash asked the pharmacist if he has any talcum powder. The pharmacist said, "Walk this way."

The guy said, "If I could walk that way, I wouldn't need the talcum powder."

A man went into a bar for a drink, when he noticed he was the only one in there. He was having a drink and eating peanuts from a bowl, when he heard a voice that said, "My, you look good today." He looked around and didn't see anyone. Shortly thereafter, he heard the voice again. "You sure have a nice-looking suit on." Again, he looked around and saw no one. He asked the bartender, "Where is that voice coming from?"

The bartender said, "Oh, the nuts are complimentary."

A lady pulled up in her car and asked the service station attendant if they had a restroom. The attendant thought she said, "whisk broom".

He said, "No, we don't. But, if you back up here to the air hose, I'll blow it out for you!"

I went to a boxing match and a hockey game broke out.

"But, sir, we do not refer to our sales technique as a snow job."

A guy got on an airplane and asked to be seated in the rear. The stewardess asked why he wanted to sit in the back of the plane. The guy said, "Well, I've never heard of a plane *backing* into a mountain."

Two guys were playing golf, and just as they were about to putt, a funeral procession went by. Both golfers stood quietly with their hats over their hearts until the procession had passed.

A stranger who was playing golf with the men said, "That was a very nice thing for you fellas to do."

One of the golfers said, "Yes, come next July, that lady and I would have been married 42 years."

1st guy: "I left my job because of something the boss said."

2nd guy: "What did he say?"

1st guy: "You're fired!"

I went to a party last night. I've never seen so many women screaming and pushing and shoving and partying in my life. I'll tell you, that's the last Tupperware party I'll ever go to!

Two guys were walking by a casket when one says to the other, "He looks good, doesn't he?"

The other guy says, "He looks dead to me!"

A police officer pulled two guys over for speeding. He handed the driver a ticket, then reached out and hit him right in the mouth. He then went to the other side of the car, reached in and hit the passenger in the mouth.

The passenger said, "What did you hit me for? I didn't do anything!"

The cop said, "I knew you wouldn't get a mile down the road before you would have said, 'I wish he would have hit me like that!'"

A hillbilly was talking. He said, "I wonder what our son John needs with three feet. I got a letter from him yesterday, and he said he had grown another foot."

A kid asked his mom, "Is it true what the Bible says, ...*dust to dust*....?" She said, "Yes, it is." The kid said, "Well, I just looked under my bed, and someone is either coming or going."

There's a new deodorant on the market called, GONE. You spray it on and you disappear. Then everyone stands around and says, "I wonder where that smell is coming from."

Two cannibals were eating a clown. One turned to the other and said, "Does he taste funny to you?"

They've invented a new drink. You take tomato juice, Tabasco sauce, vodka, and strawberry Jell-O and mix them together. It's called a BLOOD CLOT!

A guy was telling his buddy, "My wife gripes all of the time."

His buddy asked, "What's she griping about?"

The guy said, "She was wantin' a washer and dryer. So, I finally gave in and bought her a set. But she's still griping. Now she's wantin' electricity and runnin' water!"

Have you heard about the new drink called the BLOCK AND TACKLE. You take one drink, walk a block, and tackle anything.

A cross-eyed guy on a bicycle runs into a lady on the street. He says, "Why don't you watch where you're going?"

The lady says, "Why don't you go where you're watching?"

It was *so* cold last night, I saw a dog chasing a rabbit, and they were both walking.

1st guy: "What kind of suit is that you're wearing?"
2nd guy: "It's a seersucker. Sears sold it, and I'm
            the sucker that bought it."

A traveling salesman was going to stay all night at a farmhouse. The farmer said, "You can sleep with the baby or you can sleep in the barn."

The salesman said, "I'll sleep in the barn."
The next morning, he got up and there was a good- looking girl in a pair of short shorts. He said to her, "Who are you?"

She said, "I'm the baby. Who are you?"

He said, "I'm the darn fool that slept in the barn."

I read in the paper where a 24-year-old girl was suing an 84-year-old man for breach of promise. Now, I wonder what an 84-year-old man could promise her?

Dolly Parton is in a new movie called <u>Romeo and Juliet</u>. She doesn't act very well, but she sure can hang over that balcony!

The sergeant was giving his parachute team instructions. He said, "Jump out, count to three, and pull your ripcord. If your chute doesn't open, pull the emergency cord. The chute will open, float down, and there will be a truck waiting at the bottom to pick you up."

So, two guys jumped out at the same time. They pulled their ripcord and nothing happened. They pulled the emergency cord and nothing happened. One turned to the other and said, "That lying son of a gun. I'll bet there ain't even a truck waiting down there."

A guy was stranded on a deserted island, when he looked up and saw a good-looking girl swimming up to shore towards him.

She asked, "How long has it been since you've had a cigarette?"

He said, "A long time!"

So, she unzipped a pocket on her wet suit and handed him a pack of cigarettes.

She asked, "How long has it been since you've had a candy bar?"

He said, "That's been a long time, too!"

She unzipped another pocket and gave him a candy bar.

She asked, "How long has it been since you've

136

played around?"

He said, "Don't tell me you've got a set of golf clubs in there!"

You can pick your friends, and you can pick your nose, but you can't pick your friend's nose.

A hearse was driving down the street, when the back door came open and the coffin fell out and rolled into a drug store. The lid on the coffin popped open, and the guy inside sat up and said, "Do you have anything to stop this coffin?"

A farmer was telling a friend about losing his coon dog. He said, "I could set a board out on the front porch and ol' Blue would go get a coon the exact length of that board. The other day, Ma put the ironing board on the front porch, and I haven't seen ol' Blue since!"

A little old cowboy went into the bar for a drink. When he came out, someone had painted his horse green. All bowed up, he went back into the bar and said, "Who is the no good, yellow-belly that painted my horse green?"

A mean-looking cowboy, about seven feet tall, stood up and said, "I did. What about it?"

The little old cowboy said, "Well, I just wanted you to know the paint was dry and ready for a second coat."

1st guy: "I caught a seventy pound bass."

2nd guy: "What did you catch him on?"

1st guy: "A twenty pound minnow."

1st guy: "My brother thinks he's a dog."

2nd guy: "How long has he thought that?"

1st guy: "Ever since he was a puppy."

Two guys fishing on the lake were catching tons of fish. One said to the other, "We need to mark this spot. Let's put an X in the bottom of the boat."

The other guy said, "That's stupid! We might not rent this boat next time!"

1st guy: "I had a guy try to pick my pockets."

2nd guy: "What happened?"

1st guy: "Well, I had holes in my pockets, so I
          couldn't keep any money in them.   When he
          ran his hand in my pocket......................

2nd guy: "What happened?"

1st guy: "I just stuck my hand in the other pocket
          shook hands with him."

Back in Noah's days when it rained forty days and forty nights, Kansas got half an inch!

My uncle has a new hairdo. He parts it from ear to ear. He combs the front part forward and the back part backward. I asked him how he liked his new hairdo. He said, "I like it pretty good, but I get tired of people whispering in my nose."

The traffic was slow in the city. People were sitting for hours. Cars were backed up for miles, when a lady stuck her head out of the window and said, "I need to get through! I'm gonna have a baby!"

A guy shouted, "Why in the world did you get in this traffic in that condition?"

She said, "I didn't!"

One guy asked the other guy, "How did you get those black eyes?"

He said, "Last Sunday, in church, we all stood up to sing, and the hefty lady standing in front of me had her dress caught in her bottom. So I reached over and pulled it out for her..........and she turned around and hit me in the eye!"

"Well, how did you get the other black eye?"

The guy said, "I thought she wanted it in there, so I put it back. And she hit me again!"

1st guy: "It was chilly last night, so I built a fire in the

living room. And boy, it made my wife mad!"

2nd guy: "Why would that make her mad?"

1st guy: "We don't have a fireplace."

My girlfriend looks like a million bucks. When she walks, you can see right where the loose change is hanging.

A farmer took his team and wagon into town to buy supplies. He thought, while I'm here, I think I'll buy some new clothes, put them on, and go home and surprise Aunt Martha. So, he bought a new outfit, loaded up the wagon, and headed home. On the way, he crossed a creek and said to himself, "I'm gonna take a bath in that creek, put on my new clothes, and go home and surprise Aunt Martha." He took his old clothes off, threw them in the creek, and watched them float away. Just as his old clothes were out of sight, something spooked the horses, and they took off with the wagon and his new clothes. He was standing there in his birthday suit when he said, "Well, I guess I'll just walk on home and surprise Aunt Martha anyway!"

1st guy: "My brother thinks he's a chicken."

2nd guy: "Have you taken him to a doctor?"

1st guy: "No, we need the eggs too badly!"

My folks are in the iron and steel business. My mom irons all day and my dad steals all night.

A little boy climbed upon his grandpa's knee and said, "Grandpa, make a sound like a frog."

Grandpa asked, "Why do you want me to make a sound like a frog?"

The little boy said, "Because I heard Mama and Daddy talkin', and they said as soon as you croak, we're going to Disney World."

Two old men were sitting on a park bench, when an old lady in her eighties streaked by in her birthday suit.

One old man turned to the other and said, "What was she wearing?"

The other old man said, "I don't know, but it sure needed ironing!"

1st guy: "I've invented a three-legged chicken."

2nd guy: "How does it taste?"

1st guy: "I don't know. We haven't been able to catch it yet."

Two guys were walkin' down the street, when a pigeon flew over and splattered one of them on the head. He turned to the other guy and asked, "Do you have any toilet paper on you?"

The other guy said, "It wouldn't do any good! That pigeon is half a mile from here by now."

A man was kneeling over a grave in the cemetery, crying over and over, "Oh, why did he have to die? Oh, why did he have to die?"

A fellow walked up and asked, "Was that a close relative?"

The guy said, "No, it was my wife's first husband. Oh why did he have to die?"

1st guy: "My uncle has been married seven times."

2nd guy: "Children?"

1st guy: "No, they were grown women."

A little boy went to school for the first time, and there was a set of identical twins in his class. When he got home, his dad asked, "Son, how was your first day of school?"

He said, "It was okay. There are two kids in our class with the same head."

1st guy: "Have you lived here all of your life?"

2nd guy: "Not yet."

A mugger was frisking an old lady in the park and asked, "Do you have any money on you?"

She said, "No, but if you'll frisk me again, I'll write you a check!"

What did the country boy say when his mule died? "Huh! First time it's ever done that!"

The high school football coach went up to an over-sized country boy and asked, "So, do you think you can pass a football?"

The country boy said, "I think I can, if I can get it swallowed!"

A man was telling his neighbor lady he was going to New York City. She said, "While you're there, do me a favor. Look up my son and tell him to give me a call. He hasn't called me in a long time."

The man asked, "What's your son's name?"

She replied, "John Dunn."

He said, "I'll do it."

He was walking down the street in New York City and saw a building that read, DUNN AND BRADSTREET. So he went in. He asked the receptionist, "Do you have a John?"

The receptionist said, "The second door to the right."

He went in the second door and met a man coming out. He asked the man, "Are you Dunn?"

The man said, "Yes, I am."

He said, "Call your mother. She's worried about you."

It's easy to find Texas. Just go west until you smell it and south until you step in it!

An old boy said, "I've always wanted a pair of alligator shoes, so I went to Louisiana and killed an alligator. Heck, he wasn't even wearing any shoes."

My country high school changed their school colors to green and yellow so the kids could wear their John Deere caps to graduation.

A guy in his mid-fifties asked a lady in her late twenties for a date. She said, "I wouldn't go with anyone who looks like you."

He decided he would do something about that. He worked out every day for six months, had a facelift, and a hair transplant. Then he went to Florida and got a good tan. He was lookin' good!

Now, he went to the same lady and asked for a date.

She said, "I would love to go with anyone who looks like you."

As he was walking up to her house, a lightening bolt hit him in the top of the head and killed him.

When he got to heaven, he asked the Lord,"Why did you let me do all that work? Why did you take me now?"

The Lord said, "To be honest with you, I didn't recognize you!"

A politician goes to a small country town to make a speech. He asks the audience, "How many people are from out of town?" Nearly 95% of the people raised their hands.

The politician says, "Well, that proves one thing. I should have made this speech out of town!"

An old country boy took the game warden to the lake for some fishing. When they reached the middle of the lake, the old country boy reached in his tackle box, pulled out a stick of dynamite, lit it, and threw it in the water. BOOM! Fish floated to the top of the water, all around the boat.

The game warden said, "You can't do that! That's against the law!"

The country boy lit another stick, handed it to the game warden and said, "Now, are you gonna fish or talk?"

1st guy: "I crossed a bumblebee with a door bell."

2nd guy: "What'd you get?"

1st guy: "A humdinger."

I knew a lady who was *so* fat, she had more chins than a Chinese phone book.

A man jumps out of the airplane with a parachute that doesn't open. He's heading for the ground when he meets a man shootin up towards him. He hollers at the guy and asks, "Do you know anything about parachutes?"

The man says, "No! Do you know anything about gas stoves?"

Two country boys were sitting in a city park counting pigeons. A city slicker, with a little cigar, came along and asked, "What are you boys doing?"

They said, "We're just countin' pigeons."

The city slicker said, "I own this park, and I'm going to charge you a dollar for every pigeon you've counted. How many did you count?"

The country boys said, "We counted sixteen."

The city slicker said, "Well, that will be sixteen dollars!"

The country boys paid the sixteen dollars and then started laughing hysterically.

A policeman came by and asked the boys what was so funny. The boys told the policeman about the man owning the park and how they paid the sixteen dollars.

The policeman asked, "What's so funny about that?"

The country boys said, "We pulled a slick one on him. We *really* counted sixty-four pigeons!"

1st guy: "I crossed a horse with a black widow spider."

2nd guy: "What'd you get?"

1st guy: "I don't know, but if it ever bites you, you can ride him to the doctor.

A boy was telling his buddy, "I tried to get Mary Jane to marry me, but she kept turning me down. I told her my grandpa was old and sick and RICH! Grandpa wasn't gonna be around much longer and was gonna leave all his money to me when he died.

His buddy said, "Did she marry you?"

The boy said, "No, she married *Grandpa!*"

A rich man, who owned a big factory, promised James if he would marry his daughter, he would give James half of the factory.

After the wedding, the man said to James, "I'll put you in the office."

James said, "I can't stand to be cooped up in an office!"

The man said, "Well, I'll put you out in production."

James said, "I can't stand loud noise."

The man said, "Well, what am I going to do with you?"

James said, "There's only one thing to do..........buy me out!"

A little girl asked her dad, "Daddy, why does it rain?"

Her dad said, "Well, honey, it rains so the flowers, grass, and trees will grow."

She asked, "Then, why does it rain on the sidewalk?"

A little boy had hold of the dog's tail when his dad told him, "Don't pull on that dog's tail!"

The little boy said, "I'm not! I'm just holding on. The dog is doing all the pulling!"

A man calls the doctor on the phone and says, "Doc, you need to come to the house and take a look at my uncle. He's really sick."

The doctor says, "I've known your uncle all my life. He isn't sick! He just thinks he's sick."

A couple of days later, he calls the doctor again and says, "No kidding, Doc, you need to come out here and look at my uncle. He's really sick!"

The doctor once again says, "He isn't sick. He just thinks he's sick."

About two weeks later, the man runs into the doctor on the street and the doctor asks, "By the way, how's your uncle?"

The man says, "Now he thinks he's dead!"

A man hired a Chinese boy to work in his factory. Two weeks passed and the man hadn't seen the boy one single time.

Finally, he went to the storeroom to try to locate the boy. The man opened a closet door, and the Chinese boy jumped out and yelled, "SUPPLIES!"

1st guy: "In the Bible, Lot's wife turned into a pillar of salt."

2nd guy: "That's nothing. In the parking lot, my wife turned into a telephone pole."

A lady in a short mini skirt told her little girl, "When we're in this crowded mall, you hold onto my skirt tail so you won't get lost."

In a little while, she looked around, and her little girl was gone. When she found her, she asked, "Why didn't you hold onto my skirt tail like I asked you to?

The little girl said, "I couldn't reach it!"

"I think it would look better on that side, don't you?"

A nurse told her hospital patient, "Sir, we have some onion soup for you."

He said, "I hate onion soup. I'm not eating any onion soup!"

Thirty minutes later, she came back and gave the guy an enema. Later on that day when his wife came to visit she asked, "How are things going today?"

He said, "Pretty good, but I'll tell you one thing. When they want you to have onion soup, they'll give it to you one way or the other!"

1st guy: "When I was in the army, I saved two girls."

2nd guy: "Really?"

1st guy: "Yeah, one for me, and one for the sergeant."

We leave our Christmas tree up all year long. The
neighbors think it's funny, but the dog likes it.

———···⊰⊱···———

The IRS man was going to visit a hillbilly. He went
twelve miles down a highway, then eight mile down a
blacktop road, turned and went ten miles down a gravel
road, which turned into dirt. He went fourteen miles down
the dirt road onto a path through the woods, then came to a
creek with a rope hanging in a tree. He swung across the
creek, went another two miles up a path, and finally came to
a little cabin.

He looked on the door, and there was a sign that
read, *Gone to the country on vacation.*

The drunk said, "I don't go to sleep anymore. I just pass out. And I don't wake up. I just come to!"

A man goes into a grocery store and tells the owner, "There's a couple out in the parking lot playing checkers."

The owner says, "How do you know they're playing checkers?"

The man says, "Because I walked by their car and I heard her say, 'One more move, and I'm gonna crown you!"

I've liked girls ever since I found out they weren't boys.

Grandma was asking her little grandson, "Where's your nose?" He would point to his nose. She asked, "Where's your eye?" He would point to his eye. She asked, "Where's your bowels?" He said, "I don't know. They keep moving on me!"

There's a new Chinese cookbook on the market: <u>Fifty Ways to Wok Your Dog</u>.

A guy buying a plane ticket said, "I want to go to St. Louis, but I want one bag to go to Chicago, another bag to Tampa, and another bag to Boston."

The ticket agent said, "Sir, we can't do that!"

The guy said, "Why not? You did it last week!"

164

A man was following a set of tail lights in a heavy fog, when all of a sudden, the tail lights stopped, causing the man following to crash into 'em.

He jumped out and asked, "What did you stop so fast for?"

The guy in the car said, "Well, I guess I can. I'm in my own garage!"

Do you know the stuff they give you in the army to make you forget about girls? Mine just started working!

A man was visiting a farm and noticed a hog with a wooden leg. He asked the farmer, "What's that hog doing with a wooden leg?"

The farmer said, "That there's a special hog. One time the tractor turned over on me, and that hog pulled me out by the shirt collar and saved my life. One time the house caught on fire, and that hog bumped the door with his snout and woke us up and saved our lives. Yes, Sir! That there is a special hog!"

The man asked, "What's that got to do with a wooden leg?"

The farmer said, "Hey! When you have a special hog like that, you don't want to eat him all at once!"

A man was walking through a cemetery at night, when he came upon an open grave and fell in. A drunk was walking through the cemetery, too, when he heard a cry for help.

The man looked up at the drunk and said, "Help me! It's cold down here!"

The drunk said, "Well, no wonder you're cold! You've kicked all of the dirt off yourself!"

A boy says to his girlfriend, "Honey, I worship the ground your Daddy's oil wells sit on!"

A lady's husband was coming home at three o'clock every morning, pretty well looped. She decided she would scare him so he would stop drinking. She bought a red, devil costume with a pointed tail, horns, and a long pitchfork, and hid in the closet. Sure enough, at three in the morning, he came home as drunk as a skunk. When he came in the house, she jumped out of the closet and yelled, "BOO! I'm the devil!"

He said, "Well, shake hands, old boy. I'm married to your sister!"

A guy reads a sign in front of the café: **All you can eat for $4.00.**

He goes in and says, "Give me five dollars worth."

A boy who had never flown before was going to fly from Cincinnati to St. Louis. The flight takes an hour, but there's a one- hour time change. He walked up to the ticket agent and asked, "What time does the plane leave?"

The ticket agent said, "Six o'clock."

The boy asked, "What time does it get in to St. Louis?"

The ticket agent said, "Six o'clock."

The boy said, "WOW! I'm not getting *on* that thing, but I'd sure like to watch it take off!"

An Arkansas highway patrolman pulled a boy over and asked, "Do you have any ID?"

The boy asked, "About what?"

A country boy walks into a city bank for a loan. He walks up to a desk with a nameplate on it that says: DEXTER COBB.

The country boy said, "Mr. Cobb, I'd like to borrow some money."

The man said, "Young man, do you know what we do with hicks in the city?"

The country boy said, "No sir, but I can tell you what we do with cobs in the country!"

I can jump as high as I ever could. I just can't stay up as long!

An old lady in a fancy Cadillac started to pull in a parking space at the mall, when a young kid in a new sports car whipped into her spot. The kid jumped out and hollered, "That's what you can do when you're young and fast!"

The old lady backed her Cadillac up, threw it into drive, and rammed his sports car, and tore it all to pieces.

She rolled her window down and hollered back, "That's what you can do when you're old and rich!"

When you get old, you lose three things. The first thing is your memory.................and I can't remember what the other two are.

A boy calls his girlfriend on the phone and says, "For you honey, I'd climb the highest mountain. I'd swim the deepest sea. I'd crawl through the hottest desert.............. Oh, by the way, I'll be over tomorrow night,____if it doesn't rain."

A couple was celebrating their Golden Wedding Anniversary. The man was crying his eyes out.

The woman asked, "What's wrong?"

He said, "Do you remember, fifty years ago when your Dad was a judge, and he told me if I didn't marry you, he would put me in jail for fifty years?"

She said, "Yes, I remember that."

He said, "Well, I'd be a *free* man today!"

I was ten years old before I found out my name wasn't "Get wood."

A boy comes home from college and finds his dad on the front porch with his head in the trash can. He asks, "Dad, why do you have your head in the trash can?"

The Dad says, "Hey, it's my head. I can throw it away if I want to!"

1st guy: "I didn't have to go to the army because of my feet."

2nd guy: "What was wrong with them?"

1st guy: "They were in Canada."

173

1st guy: "I crossed a broom with an octopus."

2nd guy: "What'd you get?"

1st guy: "An eight-handled broom."

A drunk called the police and said, "Come and get me. I'm too drunk to drive!"

The policeman asked, "Where are you?"

The drunk said, "I'm at the corner of Walk and Don't Walk."

I can always tell when it's Sunday,.................the paper's thicker.

Song Titles

Stay Out of the Wheat Field, Grandma, You're
Going Against the Grain

My Gal Ain't No Billy Goat, but You Outta See Her
Butt

Get Off the Stove, Grandma, You're Too Old to
Ride the Range

She Broke My Heart, and I Broke Her Jaw

I called the suicide hotline, and they put me on hold.

A mother and her little girl were in the grocery store. They passed a very large lady in the aisle. The little girl blurted out, "Mama, that lady is fat!"

The mother told the little girl, "She can't help it. It's in her genes."

The little girl said, "Some of it's in her sweater, too!"

I took my Japanese friend fishing, but he kept eating all of the bait!

A man fell off a four-story building and a big crowd gathered around. A policeman showed up and asked the man, "What happened?"

The guy said, "I don't know. I just got here myself!"

A man asked the doctor, "Doc, will I be able to play the piano when my hand heals?"

The doctor said, "I'm sure you can."

The man said, "That's funny. I never could before."

My brother is *so* stupid, he would mess up a one-can milk route.

The preacher tells the pianist in church, "You can play on the black keys, or play on the white keys, but please don't play in the cracks."

1st guy: "I have a date tonight with the Hershey twins."

2nd guy: "Why do you call them the Hershey twins?"

1st guy: "One is plain, and the other is nuts!"

What did the monkey say when he got his tail caught in the lawn mower?

"It won't be long now!"

If I had known I was going to have so much fun with my grandkids, I would have had them first!

1st guy: "My younger brother went to Penn State."

2nd guy: "How about your other brother?"

1st guy: "He went to the State Pen."

My brother is *so* stupid, he would mess up a two-car funeral.

I bought my son a toy Stealth bomber for Christmas.....................Now he can't find it!

Two city slickers stopped at a farmhouse for directions. An old hillbilly came walking out with a jug of moonshine and a shotgun. He pointed the shotgun at the city slickers, handed them the jug, and said, "Take a drink."

One of them tipped the jug up, took a big slug, and said, "That's about the worst stuff I've ever tried to drink!"

The hillbilly said, "I know! Bad, ain't it? Now, you hold the gun on me while I take a drink!"

"That reminds me — gotta bowl tonight."

Dolly Parton has really small feet, because *nothing* grows well in the shade!

A lady had her bedroom walls painted. The painter was going to return the next day to paint another room.

That night, her husband came home late. He didn't want to wake her and was reaching for the light switch when his hand got in the wet paint.

The next morning when the painter arrived, she said, "Come into the bedroom. I want to show you where my husband put his hand last night."

The painter said, "No, lady. I won't do that, but I will have a cup of coffee with you."

"That was a sneaky trick, Jones, telling my secretary you had to see me about an important matter and then asking for a raise."

No matter where you go, there you are!

Preacher: I 'd like to know who called the piano player a goofball!

Member of the congregation: I 'd like to know who called the goofball a piano player!